Praise for *A Wake with Nine Shades*

"*A Wake with Nine Shades* composes scenes built from a life that moves between the dream world of a somnabulist and the mindful actions that get us through our daily lives, 'but these dreams!' Whether arguing with Robert Frost or courting his better angels, Jennifer Sperry Steinorth reveals the neglected sublime that deserves a second look. Frost becomes a metaphor for the complexity of the world we're trying to make sense of, but she invites us to use all of it—the 'hard to predict weather,' discords 'together, for pleasure,' and the 'cheers...through hunger'—to dream more. Indeed, *A Wake with Nine Shades* is a billet-doux to the world we still fight for and to the better world of which we dream."

—A. Van Jordan

"A lovely debut. These poems haunt with an unflinching attention to a broken world."

—Michael Shewmaker

"'At the midpoint of the night we were allotted/ I found myself/ in dark apart-ment...' 'Sleep rent open/and I poured out.' Like only the finest poets, Jennifer Sperry Steinorth creates her own revelatory, slant language of the interior, one of disquieting, intimate estrangements, dailiness dispossessed of its easy familiarity, distant atrocities disconcertingly present. The action of her nuanced, unsettling, multivalent lines resembles the wisteria vine on the fixed frame: 'the living thing/that will pull it down climbing/ up...'"

—Eleanor Wilner

"Although there is word-play in the title of this book and throughout its alternating brief and densely fragmented poems, the play is dark. This is a book that communicates by impression, more than expression. The impression I get is that of a dance between love and grief. The partners are locked together, bound by a locked language, a shared contrast that cannot be refused. This personal dance is also set against our dark national dance of recent and older history. Yet it's all happening at once in a timeless blur. And there's a present audience, who is inclined to see this dance as bitter and beautiful and unavoidable in the same glimpse. This is real and immediate poetry, presented on the page in the moment of its passionate breath. That breath belongs to the world, but it is also starkly human. Though death is a central feature of this book, the poetry is about being alive."

—Maurice Manning

A Wake with Nine Shades

texas review press · huntsville

A Wake with Nine Shades

Jennifer Sperry Steinorth

Library of Congress Cataloging-in-Publication Data

Names: Steinorth, Jennifer Sperry, author.
Title: A wake with nine shades : poems / by Jennifer Sperry Steinorth.
Description: Huntsville, Texas : Texas Review Press, [2019] |
Identifiers: LCCN 2019013784 (print) | LCCN 2019016349 (ebook) |
    ISBN 9781680032079 (eBook) | ISBN 9781680031911 |
    ISBN 9781680031911(pbk. :alk. paper)
Subjects: | LCGFT: Poetry.
Classification: LCC PS3619.T476434 (ebook) | LCC PS3619.T476434 A6 2019 (print) |
    DDC 811/.6—dc23
LC record available at https://lccn.loc.gov/2019013784

Cover painting: *Hair*, oil on board, @ Josepg Lozano

for the lost, descending,
through and up—

Sing

   ... *the way water is sent down a spillway stone by stone so as not to overwhelm the landscape.* ...

Fleda Brown

and for Mark,
still here

Contents

CONTENTS

Self-Portrait with Perennial Shade

Slow climber—wisteria—

long the time it takes to pull
down   the ladder it's climbed up

the trellis it's scaled to send
its fetching scent aloft to catch—

what? The bee? To near what it
longs for   purples for   the blue

veins—Air—Air—The sky.
The sky swan-diving from blue

to pink to black then up-gasp
pink again   the white-washed post

the arbor warding off no rain—

The pergola. Wisteria.
The frame and the living thing

that will pull it down climbing
up. A floret. A floret

weighs almost nothing. Florets
filled with rainsip sweetsweetsweet—

I forget. I forget how
new   how new it was—how we

once sat under it   how
under it we were   how under it—

we were perfectly content

W a k e : A Sleep in Forty-Something Winks

Midway through our night's sleep
I woke to find the dream lost
My body shaken from it—salt

\ /

At the midpoint of the night we were allotted

I found myself   in dark apartment

\ / /

Half through a rocky return journey
I woke beneath a skein of geese
Three fleet deer mice scrambling o'er me

\ /

Mid through a moonless wayfaring
Thought unrelenting

\ /

Shoveling

And just when you thought
you had dug yourself out—

Rain. The cement truck
had to be turned

away. The foundation for
your ailment is

Earth. By 9 a.m. you want
bourbon. Will settle

for yesterday's coffee.
In the car to pick up

the kids you find a bill
you thought was paid.

Back home, back on hold,
you sit down to slow

the panic. You get up
and pace. You must have

prayed. You must have tangled
your mind in cobwebs

dangling from the fan blades. Don't
worry. Whatever you've lost

should be easy to find.
You've been tracking dirt

all over the house.

Infernal coo i

Nosey streetlight—
If you had a heart
I'd shoot it out

Commute

I passed the grim reaper.
He was driving a tractor
attached to a baler.

I was

in my automobile
also on my way to work,
late. He ambled along

the shoulder slow, as certain
tractors are wont to do,
intimating no rush

to snuff and so forth.

                    Or

having started the day
knowing what it would take
to get where he was going. . . .

Do not wish for confidence.

Paradigm

O Ants, delicate Ants, undertaking cardinal pilgrimage,

crossing sand-colored floors, up wall, to our unwashed china—

You chain so fine a necklace, I

admit it, I am entranced.

Infestation?—

It is a vulgar word. *Primitive lineage?*—I ought not mention—

only—your insurgence, it seems

unending; something must be done: we trace you back

to our oldest. Potted.

Plant.

And heaving it up out pours larvae, as

from a pierced bag of rice—well, it won't be the first extinction

in my kitchen.

Hauling out the afflicted pot, trailing your fever of pearls,

I know the babes remaining can't

be spared.

Even as jet-jeweled soldiers race to save their swaddled children

falls the shadow

of my husband bearing

the poison.

Moonbright snow eclipsing
Sticky shrubbery
I rouse to rabbits ravishing
the pear trees

\ /

Sleep obscures me
Like a curb 'neath seven feet of snow

Then flood

\   /

As night was yet a thickening uterus half-traversed
I found the dream detached from me
Sanguine sheets

\ /

Midway through a night astray
I lay me down in nauseous wake
A mattress with three sleepers share
The next bed over lovers quake

\   /

I wake to feast   on egg
And toast   with a knife

\/

While We Are Reefing Down the Main with Waves at Twelve Feet and the Kids Are Losing their Lunch and the Dinghy Breaks Free

on the beach it is sunny. On the beach a nursing mother says to another
how nice the breeze. An umbrella bumps the bloom of a fellow shade-maker—
the elders beneath: *pardon me—no worries—have a beer*

And somewhere further down beyond the first grassy dune   two young lovers
find each other's liquid center (taste the sweet syrup, the whole suspended fruit)
with no idea: our ship is theirs   in a dozen years.

Plow Man

A family of snowmen watch the snowplow
plow snow out of the street. A mother,
father, two kids. They know dangerous stuff
will keep falling. Or they don't.
They're snow. They shrug. Backing-up, the plow sings
its penetrating melody of hazard:
beeep. beeep. beeeeeep. It's the song of a man
paying down his truck. His name's Rusty.
He's glad to not be home. The stuff that makes
a family makes a mess. He sips his coffee.
Four in the morning and the baby's not
sleeping. Plow trucks are sleepless. The sleepless
deport sleep, peel it away with a great blade,
but the way is hard to find even with scraping.
Do snowmen know they're made of sleep?
It's unclear. Blizzard air keeps erasing.
According to subsection seventeen C
of condominium *shuffleshuffleshuffle*,
snow from the common wealth shall be detained
in designated easements: see yonder makeshift
mountain. To create makes a crushing sound.
The snow boy waves. A big happy family,
complete with angst-y teenage snowgirl texting
. . . *a nose job . . . yeah . . . it's organic. . . .*
grown by a bunch of hippies . . . dad grumbling . . .
look at me . . . lop-sided . . . hokey scarf. Cars slow to inspect
the snow happy family, clog the artery.
Snow mom sighs . . . *it's like living in a fishbowl. . .* ;
daughter snaps . . . *you're a frozen fishbowl. . .* ;
brother raves, *I want a fish! Can I have a fish?*
The driver drops the blade; compounds
the barricade. Accumulation (weather delays,
snow days) is the *shit shit shit* of shovel in slush,
back ache, the baby on her breast swelling,
bills collecting. The driver finishes his coffee,
backs into the fumes of his exhaust,

his back-up thermos just out of reach.
This is the money. How the sky keeps
falling. Eventually, they'll fall away, drift
apart—the snowmen, they'll thin—tattered scarves
like nooses loosening, coal eyes slipping.
The driver's eyelids sweep like the blade of his truck
that he drops and swivels with a joystick—
oh, he'll sleep, sleep like a snow man—come spring.

Dear Robber

Robert Frost is hard for me to get
excited about. Sacrilege you say?
But I need him now. In order to write—
don't know what—not sure how. He loved him.
My father-in-law. Robert Frost. The world
he wrote about. Educated on site.
With a drill bit. And know how. I need him
now. My father-in-law. To tell me how
to tell my husband I need him now.
To hold the world we've lost about. The loss
we love about. I write it down. Nothing.
Nothing Robert Frost about it. Nothing
even. Odd love. Nothing Platonic.
Something catatonic. Maple saplings
aren't even. Three leaves tall. Leavings. Three
leaves tall all about the base of the tree.
Not even saplings yet. Not even
saplings, yet leafing out. I pull one out
of the lichen. I loved him. My father-
in-law. I loved him fatly. I loved
his portly wobble through the forest.
Gone now. Why I kite about it. A string.
A white line between hand and flying thing.
A white line spooling out of a hand
at the raised end of a body beached.
A raised body. Reclining. A friend
I know barely. A friend I know barely
dressed on this beach has lost her father.
I take a lover. Rob Frost. Sacrilege
you say? He took his own life. My husband's
father. My husband's wife is afraid of—
what? The drill bit? A robber? The frost?
What we winter over all summer.
The hammer and ten penny nails. What is
written. What it costs.

Lines Writ on the Backside
of a Dozer Invoice

Squirrel crossed the lawn just now
Where old oak used to be
Before our home's expanding wings
Made wicker ware of tree.

No acorns now
Will fall to fill
The kits curled in his crib
But this . . .

With a little shredding
Will make nice bedding.

Sleep estranged me

        \ /

Mid-through the mourning of our lives
Upon an unmarked granite sty
Sun-steeped among the asphodel
I almost slept.

        \ /

Sleep rent open   and I poured out.

        \   /

We click   like a Tupperware lid

Over left-overs   I think

Before   the leak

        \ /

Absolute Power

I'm scrubbing
the black

insides
of our cast

iron pot—
the charred

meat
our mannered dogs

have not licked off

          \ /

I think—
as I scrub

with my hand-
eating sponge—

if they were hungrier

life
would be easier

Infernal coo ii

Hard rain, lightning
Wind—what kind of trouble are you
In— dog still wants

out

Pissed

That the dog would dig a hole excising
The roots of the budding peony just
A week after his father shot himself
In the shower
               that the kitchen would reek
Of compost steeped in the bin we forgot
To empty   leaking an acrid rot of citrus
And rosy slime
               that picture frames purchased
Years ago still hold glossy box-store memories
Lying beside the abscessed taxes
And coffee-stained bills we cannot pay

That she would gut that goddam peony
As if   left to weather it was all
Too easy   as if the garden was wanting
For nothing but rending and rage

Halfway down a drunken road:
Sirens

\ /

Astride the horse—midstream—
I dropped my pistol

\ /

Half again through ancient copse
I came to, sharpening the axe,
And found felled 'round me
all our favorite trees.

\ /

W a k e : A Week Without Weather

The first morning steals too early
from bed. The second maintains
no touching. Third slips his
hand to graze between
her shirt and waist.
Fourth: northwest,
a breast.
One
day, two
kiss slowly.
The sixth morning
she sleeps with Fury.
Seven breaks him: every
flooded basement he'll never
not know. On the eighth morning it

snows.

Below the Dam

1.   We go for a walk below the dam before the workers
      remove the dam. Autumn. Our boys ten and twelve.

Like boys, the trees are taller. The boys have begun to swagger,
but this side of the dam, like streams, meander . . .

or trampoline a young cedar stretched horizontal across the creek,
their weight suspended:

2.   Someone has written a book about marathons and preservation.
      Some leaves our boys pick up are dismembered.

      At the Marine Corps Marathon, survivors run with their dead.
      Where a portrait is ironed on to a shirt, it won't wick sweat.

Last night, almost asleep, I bolt upright: a baby cry!
Baby?—The dog. The dog in her old dream running and whimpering.

Dead to the world, the boys' long legs twist from sheets
wrung fast and damp, rife with adolescent salt-sweat.

3.   Our progeny scan the understory in haphazard sweeps—
      filling my black book with deposed leaves.

And in Germany, reconstruction continues: the Stasi papers:
sixteen thousand bags of shredded bodies.

Puzzle workers sort the pieces, an eight-hour day pinching tweezers
matching inks—and every tear unique.

4.   Radio. Route to school. Warning of graphic content.
      Interview with an injured vet and his mother.

      I waver. Turn it off. Turn it on, they say.
      Me: Are you sure? They are sure.

We bend to consider the fallen like a team sport huddle—
a few limbs above still clinging to their flags.

            He thought he was stepping sure inside the steps of the soldier
            before him . . . . . . so high he went in the air feeling nothing—

A twister of leaves funnel at the last bend we're almost there—

            His mom: When he falls now on his new legs, both of us laugh.

5.   Sometimes I help my son with his acne.
      He lets me.

Over the weekend, at the Tate, a Rothko was defaced.
Also: "It's the most peaceful era in history. . . ."

6.   Mother phones to say the old kindergarten burnt down to the ground,
       firemen to the hospital—possible arson.

Tonight we'll carve pumpkins. Scoop the guts and seeds.
The emptier the head, the safer with a candle.

7.   This morning the boys find only leaves in the live trap.

They swing out of range of the radio, shoulder their packs.

Midway through a long strange trip
Stoop sofa levitates o'er my head
Springs uncoil   canvas frays
I shake to hear The Dead awake

\ /

Mid-sleep   I go missing

A thief in   My stead

Breathing   Heavily

\   /

Half up the mountain: overlook:
A vast horizon line unspools
For whosoever wears night vision goggles

\ /

Eye

I knew a woman whose eye was plucked days after birth.
Small river wailing.

Ointment then, that lubricant, to keep gauze from sticking.

One half blinded at birth. One half to see what blinded.
See future blindings.

I know a woman whose eye, good, was taken
in adolescence. Just
before the first blood, just after.

The lids, yes, were drawn carefully back, the scoop—clean
and sharp. Was it of love she was redesigned,
to better vessel love?

A girl stands in a river waist deep, washing.
Even a girl knows rippling, a rippling *please*.

I knew a woman just before she wed.

I confess, I do not see how removal of an eye. . . .
Call me blind.

Eye that sees the certain dark. Night, a dilated pupil.
Wherein the chasm trembles. Wherein a death so
slow she'd weep to bear

and bear it again. I am lying.

I do not know if I have ever known
such a woman. How could I know. Even if I could make her shiver,
make her moan, the tongues have been cut out

that would speak of what is known.

I know a woman. I know,
a woman. On her wedding day, like any other,
she smiles from ear to ear.

What was me then I knew
Though I did not mean to

\ /

Halfway in a mental ward
Half across a dirty floor
If you have never driven your children drunk

\   /

Thigh high in the swamp muck of our lives
Bottomless

\ /

In the bend of our body's journey, I knelt me down.

\ /

In the Shower

I am brave when I say he shot himself
braver/not so brave as him
—scratch that—

there are many ways
I cannot find
my hairbrush

we are doing fine

and who wants to be around
a runny-eyed woman
anyway   I mean

it's not even my
cross
loss

father
what right have I
mid-July

dinner with
friendswhodidnotknow
and the carrot flew

right   out of her mouth

\ /

brave like a kind of skin
the crumpled shape
that remains

beside the uncomfortable
circumferences
of drain

Eve

Once I held two worlds held
one in each
hand ate from
both one blonde
one red two stems of wine
one sip at a time it
doubled my

sight it halved
my mind each
self was jealous we waged
pink wars I
pitched the cores
the seeds shook

free the dirt
was good Two New Trees grew
tangled or
was it one tree split I
wonder how many soldiers fit inside us fit
within this leafy tent
we loved Each
Adam wandering wan

and stiff in rent fatigues
but *these dreams!*
we runs gets nowhere one-two
tree-now-orchard broad limbs sweetly bowing o'er
the earth the
dirt thickly rooted no

expunging no curtailing or re-
corking the buckshot and spent shells
of Art's demon-
strative Artillery

Infernal coo iii

Missed the bus to hell
But just—teller smirks, *bad luck*—
better hot foot it.

Cross-country Meet

Where our son runs cross-country Norm has given up
farming, sky unclear as to whether the storm

will miss us. Plummy clouds plow over fast; runners
pummel the grass-track slow: comes the blur of flags,

other people's little long-term investments. There's ours—
way off at the tree line, walking, arm clutched to his side—

his first race—we should have been more involved.
Front runners pass in a tepid wind, filmy rain shifts down

to pool in dirt-white sags of a concession tent
where troughs of bathing hotdogs steam the spectacles

of an aunt who points with stainless tongs to vats
of condiments. The water-logged wieners are free

to runners; his brother won't get one unless we pay—
he cheers as though his hunger can cover the balance.

Gasoline Finger Reek

I thought if I could make it to the station
beside the windmill   I'd be okay

at the station I could get what I needed
to make it   the rest of the way

to the office where   small adjustments
would help   me to see (my lop-sided eye)

but I   was tuned   into the frequency:
you can get away with . . . grab . . . the pussy

an expert blade   was my mind bloody
cutting it out   I cut out   my pussy

there are places we   between legs
happen   I drove myself   until the engine

sputtering   the station   miles behind me
and then   my mother-in-law   with the red can

Infernal coo iv

Adhered to the highway:
The jet wing of a cashed crow, flapping:
                        Flapping, a crowless wing works
                        : we adhere to the highway

About Face

Washing his favorite mug
    the one with the handle that fits
        and a good smooth lip

        and considering the capricious slippage
            between happy and sad

    with soap—
        a mild, liquid, lavender-scented soap—

it shot from my hands into the tub
    of the granite composite sink
            slowly leaking to the towel
              wedged beneath the P-trap

hit the rim of last night's spectacular
    spaghetti-residued bowl

                    and broke

The Wake Again

There is a poem about the rain that fell after he was shot by himself; it was very strange weather. Everyone said how strange—*yes, yes*—for years later, for many years later: *it can be hard to predict the weather.* In the poem, flowers bloom out of season because that is what they did—the phrase is *oversoon blooms;* they were also over soon. In one draft, the summer came *premature; premature* came later. It is good to have a poem for an occasion. It is good to talk about the weather on which everyone can

agree, and did, it's hard

to predict the weather except, come to think of it, didn't it look like rain didn't it look like sun   didn't it look like it would never never snow and then like it *would* snow   yes, it looked that way right up until it snowed and snowed and snowed and the gun we knew it would   melt real fast   you can know and not know   you couldn't have known   when it got hot real fast and everything bloomed and bloomed and bloomed   as if

we knew we   knew we knew

Somewhere along the road I lost it

        \   /

Morning slept
Until he rang

If you have never found a body . . .

   \ /

I woke from the dream in which together, for pleasure, over and over
We stabbed a young, half-naked woman
With a boning knife

   \   /

Infernal coo v

Bursting at the. . . .
Seems like god forgot my zipper
Smarts this   inside
                              out

What face will you wear
All your secrets or none
Till age makes them seamless

Half up my winding vertebrae . . .
Was it . . . respectable hand?. . . that grazed?

The chaste sleep in a tower
Atop a spiral stair . . .

If you have never leapt blindly . . .

\ /

Midwaltz crossing spot-lit stage
Ribbons wound to ankle lace
I saw in dark eye upturned Grace
And lost my way and lost

\ /

At the midpoint of the vow
I woke to feed the dog
Who hungers for no food

\   /

GODDOG DOGGOD GODDOG DOGGOD GODDOG

when w hole

a ho use is

all

but d ark

and art h ri tic Do g lumbers

down   nightlight

lit   ha l l

e c lip s i n g w an w all

w it h gr eat

hul king

na me less

o   w or l d   en d owed

wit h d ark un   inked

w h at

beast's b e a s t   w akes

when   collars

sl e e p

If an Apple Were a Ravine

Walk right up
to the edge of it

Kneel
down beside it feel

the pull of it   heavy down the wind
lifting up

from it dying
off A sudden suck Oh—

thump.thump O thump.thump. Your
hand along

the lip of it   long the rough
cut tooth of it Grin a

bliss an abyss an   islet Let
the up draft lift

your hand up out   and over a way
away from

the rock   from the rock of it
aloft not

of you   not your hand hovering   No
no way   no way back   no un

undoing the un
undoing You can
cannot cut it

off your hand cannot cut it off your hand
even if you cut

your hand off   What   is that scent—
that *vanilla?*   or *almonds?* a

blue and orange bird from
almost down

down *right there!*
downdown   *right there!* over

your head   right   over your head Did you   *did you?*
did you ever   did you go there

did you nearly   did you nearly
did you near   and then and then

did you give in?

A Triste Little Tryst w/R. Frost,
select billets-doux

Dear Mr. Frost,

I hope this finds you well, in your little well. Or is it more like a mine?
I wonder if you've time to speak with me about poetry and accessibility.

I'm a midlife poet flirting with crisis. More or less.

Genevieve S

Dear Genevieve S

I've nothing but time.

Do you cook?

Robert F

///

Dear Robert,

Last night was lovely. . . . (sigh). . . .
lovely. . . .

But I don't love your poems! Theirs is an old romance—
besotted with. . . .

Or maybe they're just hard for me.

Also, I'm married. Please advise.

—G

My dear Gen,

Yes, it was.

That's fine.

Sure they are.

So am I.

R.F.

///\

Dear Robert—

Last night's snow gathering in the window screens,
your hands. How easily you slip away. The Living leave tracks
in the snow.

You left your glasses.

G

Dear Guinevere,

Do you mind if I call you Guinevere?
We could role-play "The Highwayman"—

wait for me by moonlight—
I'll come to thee by moonlight

I do a good dead guy. So can you.

F

\\//

Dear Robert,

I think of you constantly.
Do you think of me?

Make X for Yes. Make O for yes.

GSS

                                                              My dear—

                        I am very sorry. When we meet, I think only of your body
                              of work. Mine is all I have left. Everyone here is dead.
                                    There are no chairs. No ankles. No vacant dresses.

                           To embrace the living, dead, is not living. To embrace
                                            the dead, living, is yet living.

                                  Earn your living. Earn your debts.

                                                              Yours,
                                                                F

                                                              /\\/

Dear Robert,

I confess I am confused by the resignation, *Yours,* at the end of a letter,
particularly a letter not addressed to the beloved. Though I suppose it is as
oddly intimate as calling a stranger *Dear* . . .

I only receive such letters from men for whom I have great fondness,
boundless gratitude and on whom I can make no claim.

I can't see you anymore.

[unsent]

/\\/\\/\\/

Dear Robert,

I have never carried a milk bucket. I love my husband, but he doesn't love poetry. Not even a little. When you look in my eyes, do you see a woman? Or a poem? What does the woman want? A poem? I can only be seen when my household is asleep. Also, he doesn't dance. Fuck Billy Elliot. And Tom Eliot. Fuck Billy Yeats and Billy Collins and fuck you, too—So goddam accessible, no one can get close to you.

In your lifetime were you known?

GenSS

                                        Fuck who?
                                   Please advise.

                                        yR. F.

                                        \\\\\/////

R

When a woman sits on a man's lap, how many pears should they halve?

G

                                        Oh, Gen.

                                        It's over.

                                        Love,
                                        Frost

                                   P.S. Just kidding.
                                   But it's snowing here.
                                        Just kidding.

                                        \\\ /\

Dear Robert,

You scarcely speak for weeks—I think you do not love me—
then there you are in the back-door rain pleading—*write me! Write me!*

What am I to make of these moods?

Yours confused,

GSS

/\ /\

Dear Robert,

Have I mentioned my sons?
Sometimes I beget. Then I worry about raising sons while bedding
Robert Frost. Pardon me putting you in third person, but surely you
realize—you're an institution. My sons have a mother who's
institutionalized.

Some people think poets are free. Is this true?

Yours,

G

                                                              G—

                                                        I'm dead.

                                                              RF

                                                        \/ \/ \/

Robert, darling—

This may sting—but I've fallen for Creeley.

P.S. I bought a new nightie.

\/

\/

Dear RF,

Which is worse— having sex w/dead men or writing poems?

                                                    Dear Gen

                                                    Difference?

                                                    Try women.

                                                                    RF

                                                    \\\\\\\ /\

Dear RF,

I love your many layers, but you keep so buttoned up—
you needn't always come so composed.

GenSS

Dear Genesis,

Better for you to undo me,
than to come undone.

Yours/ F

/\ /\ /\

Dear F,

Can you taste? What do I taste like?

G

Dear Genevieve,

I taste you in the particular only when you wear a corset.
But I've been old awhile. All the living smell the same to me.
I noticed you have nice lips . . . when you exercise restraint.
I think they are yours. But the line breaks.

RF

///////

Dear F,

How do you breach the wall between us? Must you pace the length
probing for a crumbling? Avoid border control? Dogs? And who,
after it's mussed is responsible for the wall's repairing?

G

||||||||||

||||||||/|

Dear F,

Also for *fuse*—F—

That twist of twine trespassing
bomb—that braided bit that carries
the charge whose order resends
the message. Boom.

Or to unite two twain
into one. To solder thence
to scar. I am with child. You refuse

to see me. Have mislaid (again)
your spectacles. In death, you live

outside the jurisdiction

of your arrows.

[unsent]

\/\/\/\/\///\/\/\

Dear F,

Sometimes when I call it just rings and rings.

Dear G,

I know. Isn't it wonderful?

/\/\/\/\/\

Dear Robert,

Weeks, months—watching for you—nothing. What keeps you?
I walk the field to the end of it, run my hands along the wall,
slip shod stones unclick to season the vagrant grass. Beyond
the wall, not so high as my breast, another field yields to a line
of firs. Late summer cool. Early fall. Hunting seasons. One game,
then another. Buck shot. Upflush of pheasant. The hunched blue
trees. Their blue backs.

\\\\\\\

Dear RF

I never have so many buttons as when I'm with you.

Lucite, Bakelite, mother-of-pearl, ivory, glass, bone.
And yours—so many sheathes—so long to release you.

Released, then oh— *so long,* you cry—too quick!—

                                             Dear G

                                    When I was a child
                                          I thought
                                          to swim
                                         the lake
On a shore some distance off arise dripping
                                        One afternoon
                       in secret mother sewing sisters napping
                                      a Tuesday perhaps
                                         father gone
An old man bent in a whaler
wrinkled   the water I watched
                                            the water
working itself back   to glass
Sky overcast

I disrobed

                               I crossed the dock

and quietly in   so not to wake what

it slept with. . . .   . so much sky

                             . . . . so much skin

I thought it   would take and take

a long time   I thought

and it took   a long time

until the middle   then shore

too fast   too soon

I was sad   for the lake

really   not more than a pond or

for myself

how brief my wake . . .   Did I go home

by water or walk   the shore

through reed and lily muck? The weathered dock—

I recall

sunbaked clothes

the rail tie stair   poison ivy creeping across

the path

                           And the fear of

being found before   returning

the latch

[unwritten]

[IM]

GenSS: O Lover!

GenSS: Come back!

GenSS: Take me again!

Rfrost: Oh, Gen— My dear, SS—

Rfrost: yes! YES.

Rfrost: But all the shirts

Rfrost: I left on the line

Rfrost: Are calling for rain—

Rfrost: Auf Wiedersehen!

\\\\\\\//

Dear Robert,

Before you come, I think you will not come.
After you are gone I think you will not come
again.

Please advise.

Gen

Dear Gen—

I'll see you tonight— Melody Freeze, at 8?
I'll be late.

R.F.

/\\\\\\\\\\\

Dear R—

Sometimes when I'm with you you're very old and sometimes young. Do
you feel the changing? I see your face transform in my hands from
a man of forty-five to eighty-eight to a weeks-old child—Do we live with
all our ages within us? Dying—do we pour them out till there are none?
Or wear them all at once? And this always—how long will it come
between us?

G—no idea.
Frost

/

[IM]

GenSS: Are you coming?

RFrost: Sorry, love

RFrost: Not yet— soon, probably!

RFrost: Late, as always!

RFrost: Kisses!

///\\\ ///

Dear Robert,

You are reunited with your wife. And a thousand queens, magicians,
scholars, dancers besides. And Emily and Rainy and Aunt Gert and
beloved C.D. Even you and I will be reconciled in ecstatic oblivion
eventually. Why this howling?

Was your love ever false? Did she withhold the favorite dish— serving instead a thin broth cold?

I sent love away. Was angry. My house, no longer my house, is empty. Children, husband, mother, friends— gone to the movies. A mystery. And when the culprit is finally caught—what will her sentence be?

N o t a Confession

Not another poem written in bed.
Not a poem mourning the garden

riddled with weeds. Not the sky's detached gray,
a cheap duvet over stained sheets, the tawdry

melon turned to melancholia.
Dear someone else, how goes the escape?

Do you feel for no particular reason
estranged? Do your hands ache? Is your body

a box of wrenches, a ratcheting vice?
Weeping like a child—have you made your child cry?

Please.
You do not need to tell me.

We could spend all day on this kiss. . . . oh Strange—
there could be . . . nothing . . . nothing . . . nothing . . .

but this

I n f e r n a l coo vi

Almost slept soundly.
Annoying. Almost is such
A goody goody.

Night   Apartment

The bed is	not so big
but can hold	the two not
touching	a long time
The acoustics of	his breath
in this	small
apartment that	mechanical
ka-thrum	won't
let her	forget
the fridge	still runs

Blizzard

even   as it's happening   us

in the squad car   watching the wrecker reel

our broken wagon   onto the trailer

squinting through wet gusts that make the whole of it

disappear I can't   believe it.
                    what.
                              the fact

of our accident's certain occurrence?

certain fatality briefly averted?

no. these I believe. but the opaque mass

of gray-celled drifts   the storm's fullstop   and

existential rift   snuffing eye's hold on matters appearing fixed

then proffering the handle   of vision

back again: the squad car lights   pulsing

hazards   our car   their car   wrecker   blink

blindness   a gulf   we cannot leap

Aroma Therapy

I can put lotion on my arms. I can

put lotion on my arms, dry in the fall
though today, like a summer, it's hot
in northern Michigan. And I can wear
sleeveless camisoles to work, where I drive
in my own car, though, times are tough—this—
the second of three jobs. In the car

In the car, I heard of a boy who said
NO to the al Shabab, taken
to a crowded stadium where they
chopped off his hands. After he came to

they removed a foot. I can put
lotion on my arms   here at work; I can
pick my arms up, I can pick   my arms up

and rub the gelatin into my skin.
The lipid   tincture   soothes   as it lubricates
but it's the fragrance, that sweet ambrosia
that's so intoxicating

                         \ /

The reporter tinkling through the road noise
of my Subaru is a blue Blue Fairy;
she is making the little Arab
a real, real boy. But for his wooden
puppet hands and foot—Well, it's not like he's good—
good as new—but he's planning to be

a scholar and he can't wait, can't wait
to play soccer, as they do in Sweden

or whichever Baltic they took him to.
Soccer! I think (Look Ma!) but that can't
hardly be fair: he's got no hands, no hands
for a federation ball to foul.

\ /

If the boy is a real boy, boy, he has
feelings: itchy skin at the butt ends
phantom limbs. As kids we stalked lizards
caught mostly their tails, scaly whips; a bit
a little bit horrified by our prize.

\ /

In the German tale, Pinocchio
suffers all manner of torture; the torture
makes him real, makes him cry. What do I know

of tears?—I'm no anthropologist!
Who lops the arms of a boy, shears the tarp
of his skin, the fingertips that brushed
his mother's cheek? I've got kids—get a grip!

what a grip! we say of the newborn baby
what a fine grip bringing down the machete.

\ /

Pinocchio—the original—
from the German—was a little shite—
stomping his Jiminy Cricket conscience—

Jesus Christ! But whether the loss was
tragic, I couldn't say, I couldn't say—
I've only seen the Walt Disney version.

\ /

Every species is capable (capable!)
of some kind of regeneration—
here, in this bottle, in this bottle here, is mine:

Avalon Organics for Body & Hands
with Beta Glucan and rosemary tears.
In my low-lit lobby cubicle

I keep the bottle behind the monitor,
it's got a pump-top—a sec, a sec
to work into my skin. The miracle cream

relieves my reptilian arms—but
it's the smell of pummel of pummeled
flowers that's truly regenerating.

\ /

Forgive me. I am a liar. I wept
for the boy. So? My weeping was spurred
by the smell, the smell of my comfort. So?

The boy did not dry my eyes. He's miles
away in a cold place, sitting on Danish
modern furniture the color of sand—
the color of the place he left his hands—

where his hands fell with a soft thud and were tossed
in an earthen sink with other rent bits
of soiled cloth. The boy did not press

together the nubs, the nubs of his arms
and lift to my damp lashes a handkerchief.
His life goes on and on. He reads a book.
He falls asleep. He learns to work his arms

through the long sleeves. His face, face—
his dark eyes, eyes I'll never see—the boy
whose hands—whose hands cut the boy free.

Infernal coo vii

Sideways snow over
April dog shit sometimes I
Love this awful life

R-O-T-A-R-Y

It's true   I never punched through
a door

but once I threw a phone   hard as I could
onto a futon

It bounced off the cushion
and dented   the freshly mended   wall

Someone who cared for me
had hung up   abruptly

Believe me when I tell you I am not a violent person
I was going to be

a mother   I had been talking to
my mother

I was telling her the way it was going to be

It was a cordless phone

which made it easy

Kids today don't know what it means to hang up the phone

I tell my son   *Hang up the phone.*
what?

Hang up the phone.
He blinks

Noah. Push the button and end the call.
Oh.

In the days of rotary dials   wall-mounted   with spiral cords
a thrown phone

could result in painful boomerang
I thought my mother was wrong but I changed

my plan   Maybe someday   in spite of me
my sons   will call me

Midway through the birth
I felt the hook

\ /

With wounded man and swaddled babes
In dark thicket bearing
No blade

\ /

Midway through a double-shift, a triple-shot, a single-pane

\   /

Midway through a fission trip
Lover dipping o'er my lips
I woke to see   the man a wolf
The wolf a child   the child death

\ /

Septic backed into the cellar again;
the garden half-tilled.
Neighbor backed over the mailbox again;
it won't stop the red-letter bills.
Hours— our son waits on the stoop,
his dry hook and tackle.
Our negotiations are not presidential.
We hold no office
if office means chair
in a room someone else cleans.

So haul in the shop-vac,
reschedule the tiller,
right the post,
stare down the stack
send the boy for ice-cream—
his couch-found nickels.
Then, in search of a hammer—
a weeks-old bunny behind the plywood—
blood-slick fur:
a narrow escape: the neighbor's cat.
Of the reasons to crush him, pick one:

mercy   or revenge:
on behalf of our ruined pastries:
the berryless tarts.
Creature cupped in our hands,
his terrified heart
set down in the shade behind the dogwood;
next morning he's dead in the gravel,
feeding the flies.
So call to the boy—
tall as a shovel—
point him toward the order;
there's a half-dug hole
he and his brother been filling
with time.

Ordinary Sheers

Scarlet O'Hara refashioned herself:
a gown of emerald velvet curtains,
flanking book-length, drawing room windows,
the twisted tassels looped in loose embrace
'round her corseted waist, dark locks festooned
with smart, pleated hat and verdant plumes—
her "tragedy" now iconography.

In our rooms, Love, there are only sheers:
gauzy raiment of dingy lace that whimpers
in faintest breeze, obscuring nothing
but the hard edges of trees in winter.
Anyone out in the dark could see us
wielding small cruelties, together
and apart—it doesn't make us stars.

I n f e r n a l coo viii

Both hands torn thorn raw—
Only fools go on tending
Roses without gloves

Wake in the Woods

Early in the morning
she barks at me

        They built a house in the woods

The dog and her thirteen winters

        A glass-faced house in the woods

     They moved up from Chicago
     knowing no one

        Not even the woods

A beautiful house they wanted

        With beautiful copper roofs

Angular   Jupiter   Mars in your eighth house
Seams with a silver needle
With a long   silver thread

                cancer blooms in his chest
                behind his heart
                the man will die

           snow falls in the night
              inside   poinsettia

And the woman's face: tree limbs
Bowed in the heavy snow

And the man's face: light
Light-filling

    And chemo

                           old dog

                        lying down

                        and getting up

And your father
Gone this first winter

        heavy
                   tracks in the snow
      punch
             un-
     steady

           holes

And the teacher I love
The teacher waving from her porch on 8th Street

Gray with the new white railing
Gray and the sickle moon rising

And the teacher's scooped womb
And the teacher's red-handled snow shovel

Red—

that it might be found
in what fell

in the night

. . . sleeping dog I dream
of the teacher and
her treatments

lioness at the barbershop
moonlit face

My teacher
Your father
Chicago in the woods

And the house we built with slender
needle silver thread

Can't we just sit a while?

The dog is barking

Can't we sit?

Dog   whose hips   like rusted battle armor

13th century

15th century

The pocket knife of a father

in the pocket of a son's jeans rusting
in the wash

salt the walks

Sentient
Twixt window sheer
And sash
I felt a draft
And touched the glass

\ /

Half up the trunk of virgin pine
Lightning cleaved her ribcage wide
And bent half back again to earth
One part to pray   the other curse

\ /

Halfway through a cleanse
Sucking lemons

\ /

This Side of the Fair Grounds

Say you're one of those lucky enough
to live *the good life*—raspberry blood
in the gravel—more fruit than you can bear
and the larder stocked with jam—Say you
hammock-lounge in an August not yet exhausted—
while a Bombay cat hunts in the wood stack
and mating cardinals chirp in the firs, say
your particular sky—you're sure—is bluer
than any sea—you live by the sea!—
on a pink hill, a gray town humming the swale
between, would you say your longing is just

the longing

                                for longing?—

like leaves that green and green and green till it's time
for bed? And when the day that *will come* comes—
strange as a bruise you can't explain or
swift as a hammer swing—a once blonde curled
in her house alone, contemplating unknown
relations, arms fixed to the table she won
in a raffle, decades ago—her name
from a hat, easy as that—can you *believe*
the luck—just a buck for the paper ticket,
number 874—what will you give *knowing*
nothing you can can even the score—

What If We Wake Up Dead

what   if we plant roses beside the shed

what   if we paint the living room a muddy incarnadine

what if   we go on a diet

what if   we go to Paris

what if   the dog's ghost follows us   when the house is sold

where will we go   when the house is sold

what if   we try talking

what if   I could be nice

what if we have to move in with your mother

what if we could be honest about the weather

what if   like a father   you get up to leave the room

what if   like a mother I speak   only in other rooms

what if we redo the kitchen and you become a pastry chef

what if we move to Phoenix

what if I smash the Lennox

what   if I drive away   what is good

what   if I drive away   into a tree

what if we cross our hearts

what if we make applesauce

what if you become   what kills a father

what if I can't forgive   what killed your father

what   if the kids could see us

what   if the kids become us

what   if the kids inherit everything

Wake & Island

pressed between blue pages a few hours
on our old boat which is not ours my leg
over the bow you in the stern with the kids
in the stern I'm reading poems you're not
the sky a depression of noon wilting
on our way back from the island we did not
reach   the boys drag bits of pita through
some dip argue the last cola we are not
arguing now   I said what I thought
you said what you thought and I won it's not
nice what do you want I said and you don't know
it's been so long so long since I even
wondered you said pinned here in this book almost
no wind none the water glass like old glass
that much ripple that much distortion two
small sailboats go by portside one red-hulled
the other white it's not our boat your
father's gone   days don't get more beautiful
than this the white hazed blue a few big clouds
we could not   stand it   any bluer and
the land rolls up away the glass the glass
reflects the sky thank god thank god we
cannot see ourselves for home we're headed
nothing violent nothing shattered
glass the surface just before us always
smooth always untouched and when we
mar it it repairs itself   with no help   from us

The cup tipped half one way

Then the other   which is to say

We were at sea   awake

Alone   with what spilt

\   /

And afterward we were not sure   If we had come to the center
Of ourselves by which I mean   The coming and
Going between   Rooms our sheer
Curtained rooms only   We knew each
Other's beauty   Was beast

\ /

77

Range

When one braids together
a horse
and a fence

it isn't pretty:
mangle of mane and wire, twisted legs
cedar splints. Once

on a hill
in a far country
I watched some horses across a dust road

break free.
One cantered up the rise to me
like a dear friend, long removed, glimpsed

unexpectedly
in a city to which neither of us
belonged.

We approached each other un
tethered.
He bent his forehead

to my lips, nuzzled my chest;
I stroked his neck.
All afternoon

we walked the dale, along the river
into the forest. At dusk
we lay down

beneath a clutch of trees, in the sorrel and clover
until a child—tattered dress
frayed plaits

nearing hysterics for her lost companion—
fell upon us.
Consoling herself

she led him away under the stars.
Even the fiercest
cruelest fence

is nothing
to this darkness littered
with unstrung

lights.

Lily Wakes

If you have slept long and woken slow
in your own bed   damp

with a husband   and troubles
who yet sleep and

with a longing that has no place
it would rather be

roll gently away   so as not to wake them
towards the prayers

on your nightstand   Swim there   After
half an hour

(several slow lily wavers) your husband may sift up
out of sleep

like silt   where a large fish   parts the reeds
at pond bottom

fasten his arm about your waist
a worm about

a hook like the hook you cast out skewered
and drew back

in the close mouth of a turtle
in grade school

You did not mean   to hurt him
It hurts

to withdraw the barb from a mouth   pond blood
greening your hands

Now if the man bows his head to bare   skin between your blades
where wings   had you wings

would be   before pendulum-sifting back to sleep

silt darkly settling   water clear   Why
would you ever fly

from here   why
into that terrible blue expanse

of any god

Blue Bird

Maybe snow is falling
of small world
have been shoveling
or splitting
against the close
Your lower back aches
you lie
kneading his intention
of an old door
he wants in
a scarlet cushion
and the bird
slows her flapping
twin cages
a tympani
double cell
a moment
designed

across the gray
Maybe you are tired
for hours
wood and stacking it
white wall
no matter which way
whimpers like a small dog
into the stiles
he wants out
Your tongue is a sleeping cat
your mouth
in your chest
between the locked
her solo beating
in the knit
She settles
a moment
common

and singular
perch

Lullaby for T e n o r

end table table lamp lamp light light spills light
spills our bedroom
into the hall blues the boy's gibbous shoulders—
happy? he is
hard hard to tell his face in shadow

his is the hall
underground stream tumbling from room
to room sloe and
deep his *goodnight*— a sheet, Love, we're
already tucked

in

Infernal coo ix

Music trumps sleep. No use
Calling the police. The party
Is spring
                    frogging . . .

A Door

Adore
the word
pond

It has
soft sides
It's still

like *heart*
closes
like *time*

It doesn't
contain
flood can't

be broken
by sigh
A pond

would fit
inside
my palm

if palms
could hold
like eyes

Peeled back: the eye of hurricane:

\ /

Halved and through the shovel: snake:

\   /

In dark— the middle sleep
—from sleep—

twisting

Notes

"W a k e : A Sleep in Forty-Something Winks" is after Caroline Bergvall's "VIA (48 Dante Translations) mix w fractals," of course Dante, and with thanks to Karen Brennan. "The Dead" refers to The Grateful Dead.

"Absolute Power" is after Eleanor Wilner.

"Below the Dam" is for my sons.

"E y e": More than 200 million girls and women today have suffered female genital mutilation. See *Female Genital Mutilation/Cutting: A Global Concern*, UNICEF, 2016, https://www.unicef.org/media/files/FGMC_2016_brochure_final_UNICEF_SPREAD.pdf.

"A Triste Little Tryst w/R. Frost, select billets-doux": In "The Highwayman" by Alfred Noyes, the heroine sacrifices herself in a vain attempt to save her lover from being slain en route to meet her. Her ghost lives on. Noyes's poem is also featured in an ill-fated liaison between Anne and Gilbert in the *Anne* series by L. M. Montgomery.

"R-O-T-A-R-Y" is for mothers, the cord.

"Wake in the Woods" is after Jean Valentine. It is written for Sandra and Dennis, Fleda Brown, and for Mark. And for Paul.

"R a n g e" is for far-flung dears. May we go on finding each other.

Acknowledgments

To the editors, readers, and sponsors of journals who first housed these poems, I give my sincere thanks:

Bateau: "Self-Portrait with Perennial Shade" and "Pissed"; *Beloit Poetry Journal*: an excerpt from "A Triste Little Tryst w/R. Frost, select billets-doux" and "The Wake Again" as "The Score Again"; *The Boiler*: "Lines Writ on the Backside of a Dozer Invoice"; *Boxcar Poetry Review*: "Dear Robber"; *Border Crossing*: "Dear Collar"; *Chiron Review*: "Gasoline Finger Reek"; *The Colorado Review*: "Eve"; *The Connecticut River Review*: "Below the Dam"; *The Collagist*: "Ordinary Sheers"; *Connotation Press: An Online Artifact*: "Wake: A Sleep in Forty-Something Winks"; *Damselfly*: "Bluebird" as "The Space A Body Takes"; *Four Way Review*: "Wake & Island" as "Water and Island"; *The Journal*: "Night Apartment"; *Jubilat*: "If An Apple Were A Ravine"; *The Louisville Review*: "In the Shower"; *The Massachusetts Review*: "Range"; *The Mississippi Review*: "Lily Wakes" as "Lily Wavers"; *Michigan Quarterly Review*: "Shoveling"; *New Ohio Review*: What If We Wake Up Dead"; *No Tokens*: "R-O-T-A-R-Y"; *Poetry Northwest*: "Commute"; *Sycamore Review*: "Wake in the Woods"; *Quarterly West*: "This Side of The Fair Grounds," "Aroma Therapy," "Absolute Power," and "Paradigm"; *Tar River*: "Blizzard"; *Up North Lit*: "Eye."

Infernal Coo's I–III and VI–IX first appeared in the limited addition artist book *Infernal Spits,* designed and produced by the author.

"This Side of The Fair Grounds," "Aroma Therapy," "Absolute Power," and "Paradigm" were selected by Tarfia Faizzulah in awarding the Writers @ Work Conference Fellowship. Deepest thanks to Tarfia for her belief in those poems, wisdom shared, and friendship. My gratitude to Writers@ Work for space to connect and to the kindred spirits there met.

"Below the Dam" was selected by Penelope Pelizon to win *The Connecticut River Review* Poetry Prize. To Penelope and The Connecticut Poetry Society, my sincere thanks.

To those who run and fuel The Bear River Writers Conference, whose shelter and fellowship has fed me for nearly a decade, and to the family I found there, especially Keith Taylor, Carrie Tebeau, Scott Beal, Ellen Stone,

Karin Killian, David Hornibrook, and Tim Tebeau, thank you, from the bottom of my heart. And to A. Van Jordan who opened the door. . . .

To Ellen Bryan Voigt, poet and person, for creating *A Room* . . . where there was none. . . .

For my Warren Wilson family, ever expanding, especially Gabrielle Calvocoressi, Daisy Fried, Maurice Manning, Alan Williamson, Eleanor Wilner and Debra Albery . . . my love and thanks.

For boundless encouragement and brilliance in word and deed, my love and thanks to Fleda Brown.

To those whose wisdom and attention influenced, championed, sheltered me, body and poem, including those already named and Jack Ridl, Fay Dillof, Terry Blackhawk, Chris Dombrowski, Holly Wren Spaulding, Rebekah Jarvis, Michael Delp, Liza Flum, Marie Silkeberg, Catherine Turnball, Teresa Scollon, Anne-Marie Oomen, Todd Mercer, Anne Waldman, Michael Sharick, Nathan McClain, Eric Daigh, Morris Collins, Elizabeth Sperry, Jack Driscoll, Diane Wakoski, Martha Rhodes, Dean Bakopolous, Michael Schmeltzer, Christopher Young, Amy Young, Lara Egger, Jenny Robertson, Sharon Randolf, Jenn Givhan, Will Sperry, Laura Mauer, Avra Elliot, Jennifer Yeatts, Gretchen Carr, Joseph Lozano, Melissa Fournier, John Mauk, Thomas Lynch, Stephanie Slawnik, Chad Pastotnik, Karin McCadden, Terry and Michelle VanKleek and to dear ones years removed, but not forgotten, my love and sincerest thanks.

Thank you to my students, who are also my teachers.

To Interlochen Center for the Arts, my teachers, colleagues, and especially my fellow alums, my love and thanks.

Time at Vermont Studio Center was important to the shaping of this manuscript; time at the Sewanee Writers Conference helped this book find a home. My deepest thanks to these institutions and to dear friends there met, fellowship ongoing.

Thank you to The Colrain Conference, The Grind, Interlochen Public Radio (Aaron Stander), Landmark Books, Horizon Books, Brilliant Books, Michigan Writers, and to The Workshop That Shall Not Be Named.

To Lisa Tremaine, all the folks at Texas Review Press, and especially to J. Bruce Fuller, I cannot adequately express my thanks.

To my parents, who said *YES* to art from the beginning and all the way through—my deepest love and gratitude.

To Lee, for taking us in.

To Simon and Noah, that you may create and yield to your heart's desire.

And to Mark, the long road, with love, always. . . .